THE HOT AND BOTHERED AIR BALLOON

The Hot and Bothered Air Balloon is a therapeutic story about feeling stressed. In the story, a hot air balloon is so hot and bothered that he is stuck high up in the air. With the help of a friendly puffin, the hot air balloon is able to come down to earth feeling better and more relaxed. The story teaches children about how we can use relaxation and mindfulness techniques when we are feeling stressed, and the benefits of finding an outlet for our emotional distress. This beautifully illustrated storybook will appeal to all children, and can be used by practitioners, educators and parents as a tool to discuss the importance of relaxation, therapeutic outlets and dealing with stress.

Juliette Ttofa is a Specialist Senior Educational Psychologist with 15 years' experience working with children and young people. She specialises in supporting resilience and well-being in vulnerable children.

Julia Gallego is a picture book illustrator and designer, and a graduate of the Manchester School of Art.

For Cara
X

First published 2018
by Routledge
2 Park Square, Milton Park, Abingdon, Oxon OX14 4RN

and by Routledge
711 Third Avenue, New York, NY 10017

Routledge is an imprint of the Taylor & Francis Group, an informa business

© 2018 Juliette Ttofa

Illustrations © 2018 Julia Gallego

British Library Cataloguing-in-Publication Data
A catalogue record for this book is available from the British Library

Library of Congress Cataloging-in-Publication Data
A catalog record for this book has been requested

ISBN: 978-1-138-30902-9 (pbk)
ISBN: 978-1-315-14324-8 (ebk)

Typeset in Calibri
by Apex CoVantage, LLC

The Hot and Bothered Air Balloon

A Story About Feeling Stressed

By Juliette Ttofa

Illustrated by Julia Gallego

Routledge
Taylor & Francis Group

LONDON AND NEW YORK

The hot air balloon hung high in the dusky sky like a light-bulb that wouldn't switch off.

He could not get down – he was too hot and bothered.

Each time he tried to speak, instead, he would breathe out fire like a dragon and climb higher and higher, rising nearer and nearer to the sun.

2

Birds flew away from him.

Clouds stayed out of his way.

Even the rain stopped in its tracks.

The poor hot air balloon was stuck.

3

"Why don't you try letting out some of your air?" suggested a plucky little Puffin on his way south.

So the sad hot air balloon took a deep breath in "1…..2……3….." and breathed out some air slowly, "1…..2……3…..4…..".

It worked. The balloon shrank and sank slowly.

"Good!" squawked the Puffin. "Keep going! In…1….2….3…Out…1….2…3…4… In…1….2….3… Out…1….2….3…4…"

"Now, why don't you sip some of my cool water?"

So the grateful hot air balloon took a slurp from the Puffin's flask, "Gulp!"

And some of the balloon's fire fizzled out. The balloon collapsed some more and dropped down.

"Good!" declared Puffin. "What about closing your eyes and imagining you're in a lovely, peaceful place?" suggested Puffin.

So the hot air balloon closed his eyes and imagined he was on a desert island by the sea.

He breathed in the sweet-smelling air. He heard the waves lapping on the shore. He gazed at the dappled sun-light on the sand. He felt the warm sea-breeze on his face. And he tasted the salty sea-spray on his tongue. He remembered his holiday and felt happier.

"This is bliss!" sighed the hot air balloon, emptying more hot air out of the balloon.

"Now squeeze your body tight and then let it go all floppy," whispered Puffin.

So, with his eyes still closed, the balloon did as the little Puffin asked.

He felt very relaxed,
but something was still bothering him.

"Would you like a hug?" asked the friendly little Puffin.

The hot air balloon nodded and felt the Puffin's soft, downy wings wrap around him and stroke his back.

Instantly, the balloon felt better.

Then the hot air balloon began to cry.

He told the little Puffin all about his bad day....

As he told the Puffin what was bothering him,

the hot air balloon circled and soared,

and he dipped and dropped in the sky –

tracing beautiful patterns

like a drawing or a dance.

After a while, the hot air balloon
noticed the Puffin had stopped flapping and was perching on something.

The hot air balloon wasn't stuck in the sky anymore! He had come to rest on a hill top.

The two friends smiled at each other feeling very relaxed and they sat on the hilltop until
the sun sank in the sky.